SWIMMING WITH SHARKS
GROWTH BOOK

A Companion to the Book
Swimming with Sharks

Surviving
NARCISSIST-INFESTED
Waters

Alena Scigliano
Licensed Psychotherapist

BOOKLOGIX®
Alpharetta, Georgia

This publication is meant as a source of valuable information for the reader, however it is not meant as a substitute for direct expert assistance. If such a level of assistance is required, the services of a competent professional should be sought. Reproduction is permitted for individual/personal use. All other uses need to request permission

Copyright © 2023 by Alena Scigliano

All rights reserved. No part of this book may be reproduced or transmitted in any form or by any means, electronic or mechanical, including photocopying, recording, or any information storage and retrieval system, without permission in writing from the author.

ISBN: 978-1-6653-0706-2

These ISBNs are the property of BookLogix for the express purpose of sales and distribution of this title. The content of this book is the property of the copyright holder only. BookLogix does not hold any ownership of the content of this book and is not liable in any way for the materials contained within. The views and opinions expressed in this book are the property of the Author/Copyright holder, and do not necessarily reflect those of BookLogix.

∞ This paper meets the requirements of ANSI/NISO Z39.48-1992 (Permanence of Paper)

081023

Contents

Introduction	*v*
Survivor, Victim, or Survivor-Victim	*viii*

FAIRY TALES & SHARK TALES

Your Fairy Tale	2
Your Shark Tale	3
Repeat After Me:	4

SWIMMING IN NARCISSIST-INFESTED WATERS

Common Traits of Pathological Narcissists	6
Common Manipulation Tactics of Pathological Narcissists	9
Falsehoods	17
Emotional Vocabulary	18
Narcissistic Abuse Stress	23
Do I Have Narcissistic Abuse Stress Disorder (NAbSD)?	26

SURVIVING NARCISSIST-INFESTED WATERS

Support System Sharables	32
What You Need to Know	33
What I Need from You	34
What You Need to NOT Say	35
Willing Yourself Out of Narcissistic Abuse	36
Evaluating Your Options	37
Boundaries	39
Is It Love or Fear?	40

THE NATURE OF NARCISSISTS

What Species of Shark are You Dealing With?	44
Narcissistic Supply	45
Narcissistic Parents	46
Other Narcissists	47

ESCAPE PREPARATION: DOCUMENTATION

Google Account Creation	51
Google & Mac Tips, Tricks, and Shortcuts	52

NAVIGATING FORWARD

Soul-Mending: Telling Your Story	57
Soul-Mending: Acknowledging the Abuse	59
Letter to Your Narcissist	60
Soul-Mending: Growing Your Knowledge and Understanding	62
Letter to Your Younger Self	63
Soul-Mending: Retelling Your Story	65
Soul-Mending: Acceptance	67
Letter to Your Current Self	68
Soul-Mending: Forgiveness	70
Letter to Your Future Self	71
Soul-Mending: Rebuilding Yourself	73
Letter to Someone Else	76
Jumping Back In: Triggers	78
Jumping Back In: Flags	79
Jumping Back In: Countertransference as a Red Flag	81

SHARK DETECTOR

Shark Detector	85

Introduction

This journey you're on is one that will bring you incredible growth and healing. Sometimes, it's difficult knowing where to start or how exactly to get to your destination. That's what I'm here for. Even though I can't be in the room with you, guiding you step-by-step through one-on-one therapy, I can give you a self-guided tour. *Swimming with Sharks: Surviving Narcissist-Infested Waters* is like a guidebook, and the *Swimming with Sharks Growth Book* is your interactive road map. Like any beautiful location you visit, you'll want some sort of map to provide you with directions from one site to another. The thing is though, if you just hop from tourist site to tourist site without knowing anything about it, you won't have an appreciation for what you are seeing. Guidebooks are essential for understanding the history and background of where you are visiting in order to truly appreciate it, learn from it, and grow from it. Why do we travel to new destinations in the first place? To enrich our lives. Use both this Growth Book and *Swimming with Sharks: Surviving Narcissist-Infested Waters* as your complete guide to making the most of your journey and enriching your life to the fullest! When you see this **Growth Moment** icon in *Swimming with Sharks*, you'll know that there is a corresponding page or activity in this Growth Book.

As with any tourist destination, there is never a specific order in which you need to visit the attractions. Similarly, don't feel like you have to follow a specific order in this growth book. Flip through and orient yourself to the resources it provides. That way, you'll know which parts of it to visit exactly when you need them. For those who do prefer structure though, the Growth Book is organized similarly to *Swimming with Sharks*.

Checklists

Every successful journey starts off with checklists! This Growth Book includes lists and other information from *Swimming with Sharks: Surviving Narcissist-Infested Waters* that have been turned into checklists to help you personalize the information to yourself, as well as new lists to provide guidance for you on this soul-mending journey.

Reflection Pages

These pages will often include prompts to help you further process through the information that you've been reading about in *Swimming with Sharks*.

Growth Activities

For each of the growth activities, feel free to use additional blank pages. The spaces provided are not meant to limit you!

Shareables
Handouts for Friends & Family

One of the most difficult parts of adjusting to a world in which you understand that someone important in your life is a narcissist, is that hardly anyone else, if anyone at all, in your life understands. And when you start throwing the word narcissist around, people don't really have a good grasp on what that means. It's also extremely frustrating to try to explain to friends, family, or even coworkers what you are going through, only to have them doubt and question you. And when they flat out don't believe you, it's hurtful. That's why I created these handouts. Not many people will actually take the time to read or listen to a book when you ask them to. So, these handouts provide a concise and quick reference for your support system to be introduced to what it means to be trying to survive a narcissist in your life.

Fill in the blanks with the narcissist's name or relationship. You are also welcome to print or email these to whomever you like.

*Any posting of this information online does require credit to be given to the book or myself.

Resources

These will be pages that include content I've created for informational purposes you can reference whenever needed.

Preparation Guide

These pages will help anyone who is considering separating from a narcissistic partner by providing some tips and other valuable information you can use when preparing to leave a narcissist.

Survivor, Victim, or Survivor-Victim

In the Introduction of *Swimming with Sharks*, I discuss the controversy over use of the terms "victim" and "survivor." I also share that, through my reflections on the various opinions over the two, I chose to use the term, "survivor-victim." Take a moment here to process through your thoughts on the three labels.

How do you feel about the idea of referring to yourself as a <u>victim</u> of narcissistic abuse? Does it feel like it disempowers you? Or does it feel like it accurately represents how narcissistic abuse has impacted you?

What about calling yourself a <u>survivor</u>? Do you feel like a survivor yet?

How do you feel about survivor-victim? Does this feel more or less empowering?

Fairy Tales
&
Shark Tales

Your Fairy Tale

In chapter 3 of *Swimming with Sharks*, we discuss the Fairy Tale Paradigm and how Fairy Tales have likely been a contributing factor to many people choosing to stay with narcissistic partners. Take some time to write the fairy tale that you were telling yourself at the beginning of your relationship or that you might still be telling yourself.

Your Shark Tale

In chapter 3 of *Swimming with Sharks*, we discuss the Shark Tale Paradigm and how these are the realistic stories we need to be telling ourselves and living out. Take some time to reflect on what a healthy shark tale would look like in your life and write the story below. If you aren't ready for this growth activity yet, feel free to skip it and come back once you are.

Repeat After Me:

*We don't expect sharks to change their nature,
so why do we hope narcissists will change theirs?*

*We don't expect sharks to change their nature,
so why do we hope narcissists will change theirs?*

*We don't expect sharks to change their nature,
so why do we hope narcissists will change theirs?*

*We don't expect sharks to change their nature,
so why do we hope narcissists will change theirs?*

*We don't expect sharks to change their nature,
so why do we hope narcissists will change theirs?*

Swimming in Narcissist-Infested Waters

Common Traits of Pathological Narcissists

The following is an extensive list of potential traits in an abusive narcissist. Some of these traits can be found in all of us at one time or another. The distinguishing factor between how a narcissist displays these traits and how the rest of us do is the longevity or severity to which they are present.

No narcissist will possess each of these, so please don't mistake the length of the list to indicate that. Many of these words will be synonymous with one another; however, I'm sure that certain ones will resonate more with one person over another. I have chosen to include so many, because having the language you need to describe what you are experiencing will be helpful on many levels, including being able to better express yourself to others as well as moving you forward on your healing journey.

Use this list to check off any of the traits you have noticed in your narcissist. If you have multiple narcissists, go to www.AlenaScigliano.com to create extra copies of the PDF version of this checklist.

199 Terms to Describe a Pathological Narcissist

Some of the traits listed can be found in each of us at one time or another. The distinguishing factor between how a narcissist displays these characteristics & how the rest of us do is the longevity or severity to which they are present and how deeply they impact others. It is important to note that no narcissist will have all of these traits. Check off the ones you see present in the narcissist in your life.

- Abrasive
- Abrupt
- Abusive
- Addiction Susceptible
- **Aggressive**
- Amoral
- Angry
- **Antagonistic**
- Anxious
- Argumentative
- **Arrogant**
- Asocial
- **Authoritarian**
- **Belligerent**
- Blaming of Others
- Blunt
- Boastful
- Boisterous
- Boorish
- Calculating
- **Callous**
- Careless
- Charming
- Coarse
- Cocky
- Cold
- **Compulsive**
- Conceited
- Condemnatory
- **Condescending**
- **Conflictual**
- Confrontational
- **Contemptuous**
- **Controlling**
- Crude
- Cruel
- Cunning
- Cynical
- Deceitful
- **Defensive**
- Demanding
- **Destructive**
- Detached
- Devious
- Difficult
- **Disagreeable**
- Disconcerting
- Discontented
- Discouraging
- Discourteous
- **Dishonest**
- Disloyal
- **Disputatious**
- **Disrespectful**
- Disruptive
- Dissolute-lax in morals
- Distant
- **Dogmatic**
- **Domineering**
- **Dysregulated**
- **Egocentric**
- Empathy Atypical
- **Empathy Deficient**
- **Entitled**
- Envious
- Erratic
- **Evasive**
- Extravagant
- Extroverted
- Fanatical
- Fawning
- Flirtatious
- Forgetful
- Frivolous
- **Gossipy**
- **Greedy**
- Grumpy
- Harsh
- Hateful
- **Haughty**
- Hostile
- Humorless
- Hurtful
- **Hypercritical**
- Ignorant
- **Illogical**
- Impatient
- Impolite
- Inconsistent
- Indifferent
- Indiscreet
- Inflammatory
- Inflexible
- **Insecure**
- **Insensitive**
- **Insincere**
- Insulting
- Interfering
- Intimacy Avoidant
- **Intolerant**

***Bold** items are the traits I've come across most often through my clinical work as a psychotherapist.

199 Terms to Describe a Pathological Narcissist (cont'd)

- [ ] Introverted
- [ ] **Irrational**
- [ ] Irresponsible
- [ ] Jealous
- [ ] **Judgmental**
- [ ] Know-it-all
- [ ] **Lacking Integrity**
- [ ] Machiavellian
- [ ] Macho
- [ ] Malicious
- [ ] **Manipulative**
- [ ] Materialistic
- [ ] Mean
- [ ] Meddlesome
- [ ] Melodramatic
- [ ] Miserable
- [ ] Monstrous
- [ ] Moody
- [ ] Mysterious
- [ ] Narrow-minded
- [ ] Nasty
- [ ] Negative
- [ ] **Neglectful**
- [ ] Obnoxious
- [ ] Obsessive

- [ ] **Obstinate**
- [ ] Opinionated
- [ ] Overcharitable
- [ ] **Oversensitive**
- [ ] Offensive
- [ ] Paranoid
- [ ] **Passive-aggressive**
- [ ] Patronizing
- [ ] Pessimistic
- [ ] Petty
- [ ] **Petulant**
- [ ] Pompous
- [ ] **Possessive**
- [ ] Power-Hungry
- [ ] Predatory
- [ ] Prejudiced
- [ ] Pretentious
- [ ] **Promiscuous**
- [ ] **Puritanical**
- [ ] Quarrelsome
- [ ] Racist
- [ ] **Reactive**
- [ ] Reckless
- [ ] Repulsive
- [ ] Resentful

- [ ] Rigid
- [ ] Rude
- [ ] Ruthless
- [ ] Sanctimonious
- [ ] Scary
- [ ] Scornful
- [ ] Secretive
- [ ] **Self-centered**
- [ ] Self-destructive
- [ ] Self-indulgent
- [ ] Selfish
- [ ] Sexist
- [ ] Shallow
- [ ] Sly
- [ ] Sneaky
- [ ] Snobbish
- [ ] Stingy
- [ ] Stubborn
- [ ] **Superficial**
- [ ] Suspicious
- [ ] Tactless
- [ ] Temperamental
- [ ] Thoughtless
- [ ] **Toxic**
- [ ] Tyrannical

- [ ] Unappreciative
- [ ] Uncaring
- [ ] Uncharitable
- [ ] Uncommunicative
- [ ] **Uncooperative**
- [ ] Uncouth
- [ ] Unethical
- [ ] **Unforgiving**
- [ ] Ungrateful
- [ ] Uninhibited
- [ ] Unkind
- [ ] Unpleasant
- [ ] Unrealistic
- [ ] Unreliable
- [ ] Unstable
- [ ] Untrustworthy
- [ ] Uptight
- [ ] Vain
- [ ] Vengeful
- [ ] **Vindictive**
- [ ] Violent
- [ ] **Volatile**
- [ ] Vulgar
- [ ] Withdrawn
- [ ] _____

***Bold** items are the traits I've come across most often through my clinical work as a psychotherapist.

Common Manipulation Tactics of Pathological Narcissists

You read about the common manipulation tactics used by narcissists to get what they want in *Swimming with Sharks: Surviving Narcissist-Infested Waters*. Here is a brief summary of each of the terms.

 Manipulation Tactic	Description
Coercively Controlling	Intimidates or humiliates you into giving up your freedom of choice and creating an unequal power dynamic.
Charming Others	Used as an extremely effective technique to draw you in as well as manipulate others in the subtlest of ways.
Deploying Flying Monkeys	Using other people to do their bidding, such as enlisting family members to convince you of something.
Devaluing	Treating you or what you care about as unimportant or unworthy.
Discarding	Gets rid of or casts you away as though you are useless.
Dismissing	Showing indifference toward you or disregarding the things you say.
Distracting	Similar to a magician—gets you to temporarily focus attention away from whatever they don't want you to see.
Future Faking	Promising something for your future together to get you to do what they want without any intention to follow through.
Gaslighting	Planting seeds of doubt or manipulating information to make you question your memories, sanity, or perception of reality.
Hoovering	Used to suck you back into the relationship by any means necessary if they feel you pulling away.

Manipulation Tactic	Description
Invalidating	Denying, rejecting, or dismissing your feelings.
Lying	Saying something that isn't true in avoidance of undesirable consequences the truth might bring.
Love Bombing	Attempting to influence you by showering you with over-the-top gifts, praise, accolades, attention, or affection.
Manipulating (Dysfunctional Manipulation)	Intentionally implementing specific tactics to get what they want for dysfunctional and unhealthy reasons.
Mind Reading	Inferring or assuming what you are thinking or feeling without bothering to ask you what it is.
Minimizing	Making your experience seem unimportant or not taking responsibility for their actions or choices.
Minimizing—Maximizing	Minimize what they do and maximize what you do, or vice versa, depending on the context.
Mirror	Professing to have the same likes/dislikes, dreams, passions, hobbies, etc., to promote a stronger bond.
Narcissist's Amnesia	Claiming to not remember their abusive behaviors.
Narcissist's Delusion	Telling a lie so thoroughly and over such a long period that they begin to believe it's true—the lie becomes their truth/reality.

RESOURCE

Manipulation Tactic	Description
Narcissist's Injury	Perceiving theirself as being under attack when held accountable for their actions—their sense of self feels threatened.
Narcissist's Rage	Intensely aggressive or passive-aggressive reaction to a narcissistic injury—irrational and disproportionate to what occurred.
Narcissistic Supply Hopping	Drains one person of their emotional energy reserves then moves on to another for more narcissistic supply.
Project	Defense mechanism in which a narcissist will attribute or assign their traits or behaviors to someone else.
Scapegoat	Unfairly placing blame on someone else for something they did not cause.
Shaming	Attempting to make you feel less worthy as a means to control you.
Spreading Falsehoods	Will lie and speak poorly about you to others in order to shift loyalty or make themselves look better.
Stonewall	Refusing to interact or communicate with you as a means to reestablish their control.
Tale Twist	Twisting someone else's words into the story the narcissist wants to tell.
Triangulate	Occurs when there is conflict between the narcissist and someone else, and they pull a third party into the conflict.
Victimizing	A form of distraction, they make themselves look like a victim to shift your focus away from their wrongdoings.

Now, go ahead and check off any of the manipulation tactics that resonate with you. Space has been left under each one in case you'd like to make notes or list examples of how these tactics have been used against you.

- [ ] *Coercively Controlling*

- [ ] *Charming*

- [ ] *Deploying Flying Monkeys*

- [ ] *Devaluing*

- [ ] *Discarding*

- [ ] *Dismissing*

- [ ] *Distracting*

- [ ] *Future Faking*

CHECKLIST

- ☐ *Gaslighting*

- ☐ *Hoovering*

- ☐ *Invalidating*

- ☐ *Love Bombing*

- ☐ *Lying*

- ☐ *Manipulating (Dysfunctional Manipulation)*

- ☐ *Mind Reading*

- ☐ *Minimizing*

- ☐ *Minimizing—Maximizing*

CHECKLIST

☐ *Mirroring*

☐ *Narcissist's Amnesia*

☐ *Narcissist's Delusion*

☐ *Narcissist's Injury*

☐ *Narcissist's Rage*

☐ *Narcissistic Supply Hopping*

☐ *Projecting*

☐ *Scapegoating*

☐ *Spreading Falsehoods*

- ☐ *Stonewalling*
  _____
  _____
  _____

- ☐ *Tale Twisting*
  _____
  _____
  _____

- ☐ *Triangulating*
  _____
  _____
  _____

- ☐ *Victimizing Theirself*
  _____
  _____
  _____

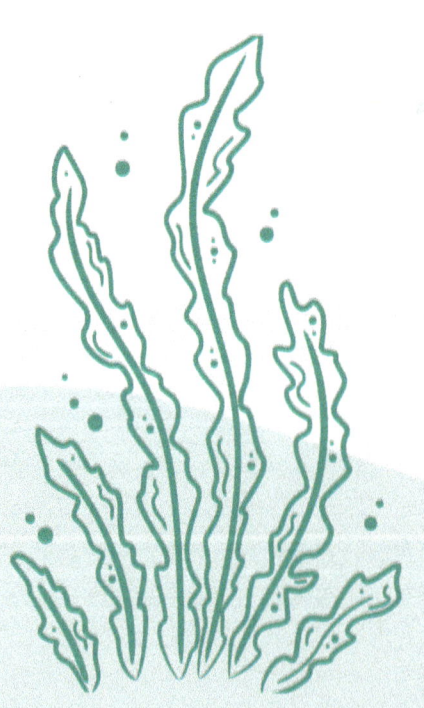

Falsehoods

As discussed in the book, narcissists often spread lies about you to others for any number of reasons. Let's process through some of these and the impact they've had.

Make a list here of the lies that your narcissist has already told others.
_____
_____
_____
_____
_____
_____
_____
_____

Describe how this has made you feel.
_____
_____
_____
_____
_____
_____
_____
_____

Describe how this has impacted your life and relationships with other people.
_____
_____
_____
_____
_____
_____
_____

EMOTIONAL VOCABULARY

It's so important to be able to express what you're feeling. To do this though, you need to be able to *name* what you're feeling. Our emotional vocabulary is critical to interpersonal connection through healthy and effective communication. In addition, it can play a vital role in the introspection that is required for healing. I remember when my counselor handed me a "feelings" word list. I had been struggling greatly to be able to name my feelings whenever she asked me to. The list not only helped me be able to fully communicate to my therapist what I was experiencing, it also helped me to be able to work through those feelings. For some reason, without the words to name them, I was unable to fully access the emotion in order to resolve it.

Use the list below to help you figure out what you're feeling whenever you find yourself at a loss for feeling words too!

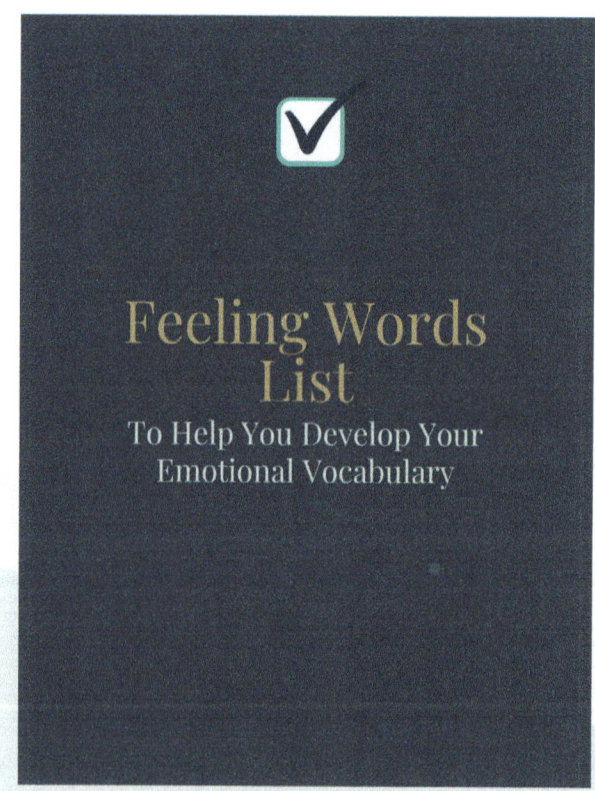

Feeling Words

Use this list to help you identify the emotions you commonly experience as a result of the narcissist(s) in your life.

ANGRY	DEPRESSED	CONFUSED	HELPLESS
☐ irritated	☐ lousy	☐ upset	☐ incapable
☐ enraged	☐ disappointed	☐ doubtful	☐ alone
☐ hostile	☐ discouraged	☐ uncertain	☐ paralyzed
☐ insulting	☐ ashamed	☐ indecisive	☐ fatigued
☐ annoyed	☐ powerless	☐ perplexed	☐ useless
☐ upset	☐ diminished	☐ embarrassed	☐ inferior
☐ hateful	☐ guilty	☐ hesitant	☐ vulnerable
☐ offensive	☐ dissatisfied	☐ shy	☐ empty
☐ bitter	☐ miserable	☐ stupefied	☐ forced
☐ aggressive	☐ detestable	☐ disillusioned	☐ hesitant
☐ resentful	☐ repugnant	☐ unbelieving	☐ despair
☐ inflamed	☐ despicable	☐ skeptical	☐ frustrated
☐ provoked	☐ disgusting	☐ distrustful	☐ distressed
☐ incensed	☐ abominable	☐ misgiving	☐ woeful
☐ infuriated	☐ terrible	☐ lost	☐ pathetic
☐ cross	☐ in despair	☐ unsure	☐ tragic
☐ worked up	☐ sulky	☐ uneasy	☐ in a stew
☐ boiling	☐ bad	☐ pessimistic	☐ dominated
☐ fuming		☐ tense	

Add any additional words to the blanks that I have not included.

Feeling Words

Use this list to help you identify the emotions you commonly experience as a result of the narcissist(s) in your life.

INDIFFERENT	AFRAID	HURT	SAD
☐ insensitive	☐ fearful	☐ crushed	☐ tearful
☐ dull	☐ terrified	☐ tormented	☐ sorrowful
☐ nonchalant	☐ suspicious	☐ deprived	☐ pained
☐ neutral	☐ anxious	☐ pained	☐ grief
☐ reserved	☐ alarmed	☐ tortured	☐ anguish
☐ weary	☐ panic	☐ dejected	☐ desolate
☐ bored	☐ nervous	☐ rejected	☐ desperate
☐ preoccupied	☐ scared	☐ injured	☐ pessimistic
☐ cold	☐ worried	☐ offended	☐ unhappy
☐ disinterested	☐ frightened	☐ afflicted	☐ lonely
☐ lifeless	☐ timid	☐ aching	☐ grieved
☐	☐ shaky	☐ victimized	☐ mournful
☐	☐ restless	☐ heartbroken	☐ dismayed
☐	☐ doubtful	☐ agonized	☐
☐	☐ threatened	☐ appalled	☐
	☐ cowardly	☐ humiliated	☐
	☐ quaking	☐ wronged	☐
	☐ wary	☐ alienated	☐
	☐	☐	☐
	☐	☐	
	☐	☐	
	☐		

Add any additional words to the blanks that I have not included.

Feeling Words

Use this list to help you identify the emotions you commonly experience or are not able to experience as a result of the narcissist(s) in your life.

LOVE
- [ ] loving
- [ ] considerate
- [ ] affectionate
- [ ] sensitive
- [ ] tender
- [ ] devoted
- [ ] attracted
- [ ] passionate
- [ ] admiration
- [ ] warm
- [ ] touched
- [ ] close
- [ ] comforted
- [ ] loved
- [ ]
- [ ]
- [ ]
- [ ]
- [ ]

INTERESTED
- [ ] concerned
- [ ] affected
- [ ] fascinated
- [ ] intrigued
- [ ] absorbed
- [ ] inquisitive
- [ ] engrossed
- [ ] curious
- [ ] drawn toward
- [ ]
- [ ]
- [ ]
- [ ]
- [ ]

POSITIVE
- [ ] eager
- [ ] keen
- [ ] earnest
- [ ] intent
- [ ] inspired
- [ ] determined
- [ ] excited
- [ ] enthusiastic
- [ ] bold
- [ ] brave
- [ ] daring
- [ ] optimistic
- [ ]
- [ ]
- [ ]
- [ ]
- [ ]

STRONG
- [ ] impulsive
- [ ] free
- [ ] sure
- [ ] certain
- [ ] rebellious
- [ ] unique
- [ ] dynamic
- [ ] tenacious
- [ ] hardy
- [ ] secure
- [ ] confident
- [ ] challenged
- [ ]
- [ ]
- [ ]
- [ ]
- [ ]

Add any additional words to the blanks that I have not included.

Feeling Words

Use this list to help you identify the emotions you commonly experience or are not able to experience as a result of the narcissist(s) in your life.

OPEN	HAPPY	ALIVE	GOOD
☐ understanding	☐ great	☐ playful	☐ calm
☐ confident	☐ joyous	☐ courageous	☐ peaceful
☐ reliable	☐ lucky	☐ energetic	☐ at ease
☐ easy	☐ fortunate	☐ liberated	☐ comfortable
☐ amazed	☐ delighted	☐ optimistic	☐ pleased
☐ free	☐ overjoyed	☐ impulsive	☐ encouraged
☐ sympathetic	☐ gleeful	☐ free	☐ clever
☐ interested	☐ thankful	☐ animated	☐ surprised
☐ satisfied	☐ important	☐ spirited	☐ content
☐ receptive	☐ festive	☐ thrilled	☐ quiet
☐ accepting	☐ ecstatic	☐ wonderful	☐ certain
☐ kind	☐ glad	☐	☐ relaxed
☐	☐ cheerful	☐	☐ serene
☐	☐ elated	☐	☐ reassured
☐	☐ jubilant	☐	☐
☐	☐	☐	☐
☐	☐	☐	☐

Add any additional words to the blanks that I have not included.

Narcissistic Abuse Stress

Are you experiencing Narcissistic Abuse Stress (NAb Stress)? Check off the reactions below that resonate with you and write in some examples of how this affects you on a regular basis.

Cognitive & Emotional Reactions

☐ *Trapped*
_____
_____
_____

☐ *Unsure and Unsafe*
_____
_____
_____

☐ *Misunderstood*
_____
_____
_____

☐ *Used*
_____
_____
_____

☐ *Confusion*
_____
_____
_____

☐ *Fear, Stress, Anxiety, Panic*
_____
_____
_____

☐ *Hurt, Depression, Grief*
_____
_____
_____

☐ *Shame*
_____
_____
_____

BEHAVIORAL REACTIONS

☐ *Taking it out on someone else*
___
___
___

☐ *Isolating Oneself*
___
___
___

☐ *Shutting Down*
___
___
___

☐ *Avoidance*
___
___
___

☐ *Secondary Narcissist*
___
___
___

☐ *Narcissist-by-Proxy*
___
___
___
___

SURVIVAL REACTIONS

- [ ] *Suppression of Emotions*
  _____
  _____
  _____

- [ ] *Narcissistic Abuse Amnesia*
  _____
  _____
  _____

- [ ] *Survival Manipulation*
  _____
  _____
  _____

- [ ] *Hypervigilant Manipulation*
  _____
  _____
  _____

- [ ] *Extreme Validation*
  _____
  _____
  _____

Do I Have Narcissistic Abuse Stress Disorder (NAbSD)?

Think you might be struggling with Narcissistic Abuse Stress Disorder (NAbSD)? Check off the items below that apply to you and compare them to the criteria required to meet the diagnosis.

*As a reminder, this is not an official diagnosis, nor is it one that is recognized by any official organization within the fields of medicine, psychology, or counseling.

Not everyone will experience each of the symptoms listed, and symptoms may change over time. Similar to official diagnoses found in the DSM-V, to qualify for a diagnosis of Narcissistic Abuse Stress Disorder, the symptoms would need to be at a level that causes significant distress or impairment within personal and/or interpersonal areas of functioning.

Psychological Symptoms

Presence of any of the following symptoms related to mental functioning:
Difficulty concentrating, frequently distracted.
Intrusive memories or flashbacks of occurrences of narcissistic abuse.

Presence of any of the following numbing symptoms:
- ⚓ Difficulty experiencing positive emotions.
- ⚓ Decreased interest in activities that once interested you outside of the narcissistic relationship.
- ⚓ Feeling isolated from others outside of your relationship.
- ⚓ Mental and emotional crash after interacting with the narcissist.
- ⚓ Neglecting one's own hobbies and interests in order to mold oneself to the desires of the narcissist. Sometimes to the point of forgetting your own interests.
- ⚓ Narcissistic Abuse Amnesia—a purposeful and sometimes subconscious forgetting of repeated abuse, or willfully ignoring the fault of the abuser in their choice to engage in abusive behavior.

Presence of any of the following fear-based symptoms:
- ⚓ Persistent levels of heightened anxiety, particularly when anticipating the narcissist returning home or anticipating them responding poorly to something.
- ⚓ Emotional distress after reminders of the abuse or the abuser.
- ⚓ Avoidance of narcissistic abuse-related thoughts, feelings, or external reminders.
- ⚓ Avoidance of allowing oneself to think of the narcissist as an abuser.
- ⚓ Avoidance of openly sharing with others what you are experiencing.
- ⚓ Excessive worrying that no one will understand if you do share.
- ⚓ Avoidance of new relationships out of fear that they will be a narcissist too.

Presence of any of the following symptoms resulting from negative experiences with others:
- ⚓ Lingering discomfort after telling one or more people outside of the relationship private details about the narcissistic abuse and then experiencing them doubting the truth of what you say. This may lead to worry and avoidance of being vulnerable in the future or with other people.

Presence of any of the following symptoms related to self-esteem:
- ⚓ Overly negative thoughts or assumptions about oneself or the world.
- ⚓ Pessimistic thoughts related to the future (i.e., anticipating everyone else will be a narcissist).
- ⚓ Blaming oneself for the narcissistic abuse.
- ⚓ Diminished self-esteem, sometimes to the point of seemingly nonexistent.
- ⚓ Questioning one's own sanity, particularly after confrontations with the narcissist.

Behavioral Symptoms

Presence of any of the following symptoms related to conflict avoidance:
- ⚓ Holding in one's own thoughts and feelings for fear that sharing will instigate conflict.
- ⚓ Hypervigilant in avoiding anything that might set off the narcissist. This includes one's own behaviors, choices, actions, communication,

and social media posts, as well as others' behaviors, choices, actions, and communication.
- ⚓ Making sure that things are "just right," whether that's around the house, with the kids or siblings, one's own academic or work performance, etc., in order to avoid conflict with the narcissist.

Presence of any of the following symptoms related to isolation:
- ⚓ Increasingly isolating oneself from others outside of the narcissistic relationship (i.e., avoiding going out with friends, talking on the phone with family members).
- ⚓ Avoiding social situations that may prompt questions if the narcissist is not present or embarrassment if the narcissist is.

Presence of any of the following symptoms related to the suppression of emotions:
- ⚓ Experiencing an outburst of feelings, erupting all at once, causing one to "blow up" at the narcissist, and subsequently experiencing shame, regret, and self-blame, which can last for days, weeks, months, or years, even if the relationship has ended.
- ⚓ Experiencing maladies or ailments within the body, which one suspects may have manifested due to the suppression of emotions over extended periods, such as weeks, months, or years.

Presence of any of the following symptoms related to aggression:
- ⚓ Impulsively becoming physically aggressive in reaction to narcissistically abusive behaviors, such as shoving the narcissist when they won't leave your personal space.
- ⚓ Aggressive and/or disproportionate responses to people other than the narcissist, such as impulsively snapping, typically toward family members other than the narcissist, children, siblings, the other parent, coworkers, or friends.

Presence of any of the following symptoms related to adopting survival strategies:
- ⚓ Survival Manipulation: Making certain choices or behaving in certain ways with the hope that the narcissist will not become enraged or otherwise behave poorly.

- ⚓ Hypervigilant Manipulation: An anxious type of survival manipulation where the survivor-victim tries to anticipate both the needs and the outbursts of the narcissist, and provide for or change the circumstances accordingly, in order to avoid experiencing any of their abusive behavior, whether it's yourself who would be on the receiving end or others.
- ⚓ Extreme Validation: Frequently going "overboard" in validating the narcissist in an effort to encourage behavioral changes in the narcissist.

Presence of any of the following symptoms related to substance use:
- ⚓ Overusing or abusing substances (food, alcohol, legal or illegal drugs) as a means to mentally escape or alleviate the discomfort resulting from ongoing narcissistic abuse.
- ⚓ Using substances when you otherwise wouldn't because of feeling pressured by the narcissist to do so and fearing their reaction if you don't.

While this proposed disorder has not yet been submitted to the American Psychiatric Association's Committee on Psychiatric Diagnosis and Assessment for consideration to be included in the DSM-V, this is a set of proposed diagnostic criteria I created to be used to identify the presence of Narcissistic Abuse Stress Disorder (NAbSD).

The criteria for diagnosis of this disorder were developed from two main factors. Firstly, they are based on my clinical experience providing psychotherapy to survivor-victims of narcissistic abuse since 2013, during which I have observed, documented, and tracked the effects of narcissistic abuse on each of these patients. Over time, clear and distinctive patterns emerged within the clinical anecdotal evidence, illustrating commonalities in the experiences of those who are targets of narcissistic abuse. Secondly, I integrated these identified patterns into a familiar framework, using the stress disorders that are currently present in the DSM-V as a model (i.e., PTSD and Acute Stress Disorder). The criteria have not been developed from any formal academic or clinical studies.

SURVIVING NARCISSIST-INFESTED WATERS

SUPPORT SYSTEM SHARABLES

Use the following *Shareables* as handouts to provide to your support system in order to introduce them to what it means to be in the midst of surviving a narcissist in your life.

There are blanks for you to add the narcissist's name or relationship, as well as blanks for you to add your own ideas. You are also welcome to print or email these to whomever you like.

*Reproduction is permitted for individual/personal use. All other uses need to request permission.

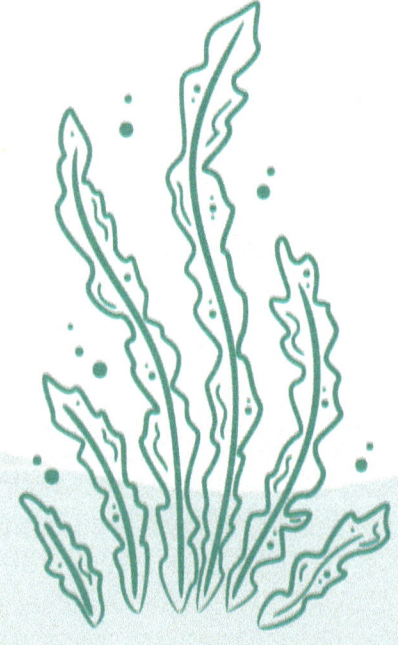

What You Need to Know

- ⚓ Here are some words to describe what _____ is like: **antagonistic, conflictual, contemptuous, controlling, dysregulated, entitled, manipulative, psychologically abusive, toxic, tyrannical, verbally abusive.**

- ⚓ Here are some words to describe how _____ makes me feel: **anxious, ashamed, broken, confused, controlled, devalued, discarded, dismissed, invalidated, manipulated, minimized.**

- ⚓ Here are some things I'm trying to do to help deal with _____: **set boundaries, go gray rock, go no contact, build my support system, rebuild my confidence and independence.**

- ⚓ None of this is my fault.

- ⚓ I do not have control over how _____ treats me.

- ⚓ _____ will try to make me seem crazy to you.

- ⚓ There is nothing I can do to make _____ change. Narcissistic people are not willing to change.

- ⚓ This is not a sickness, disease, or illness that can be cured or healed. It cannot be prayed away.

- ⚓ There is nothing wrong with *me*.

- ⚓ Just because someone is family, doesn't mean they'll be there for me no matter what. _____ is not *capable* of being there for me.

- ⚓ Just because someone is family, doesn't mean they are good/healthy for me.

- ⚓ No, God does not expect me to stay in an abusive _____ [marriage | partnership | relationship | job | friendship | fill in the blank with any other descriptor of your relationship to the narcissist].

- ⚓ No, God does not expect me to continue to be abused by my _____ [spouse | partner | parent | sibling | friend | boss | pastor | child].

What I Need from You

- Do not have expectations of me.
- Unconditional Support—Be here to support me no matter what.
- When I feel I need to leave, support me.
- While I feel I need to stay, support me.
- Do not question my choices/decisions.
- I don't have much in my reserve tank (left to give), so please just take what you can get/what I can give. Don't push me for more.
- Tammy Wynette's "Stand By Your Man" (or woman/person), is not my ode/theme song. Do not quote it to me.
- Help me with the kids.
- _____
- _____
- _____
- _____
- _____

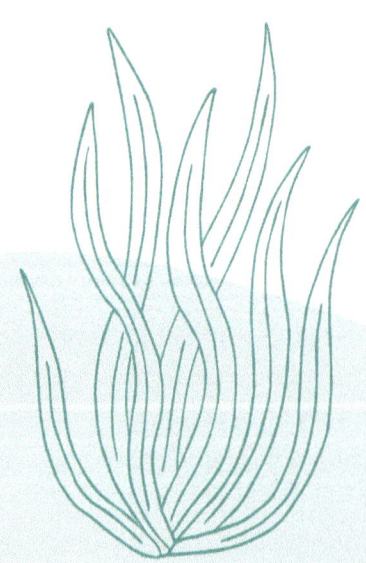

What You Need to NOT Say

- ⚓ Are you sure?
- ⚓ What did you do to make them . . . ?
- ⚓ What is your part in the conflict?
- ⚓ What could you have done differently?
- ⚓ He/she/they can change.
- ⚓ But she's your mom/he's your dad.
- ⚓ But they're family. You have to stick by them no matter what.
- ⚓ They're the only ones who will be there for you no matter what.
- ⚓ But you took a vow to stick by them in sickness.
- ⚓ If you get divorced, you will go to Hell.
- ⚓ Think of the kids. How will this hurt them?
- ⚓ You'll never find someone else like them.
- ⚓ But how will you provide for yourself financially?

Types of Statements to Avoid

- ⚓ Anything related to God or religious perceptions of obligation.
- ⚓ Anything that is shame or guilt-inducing.

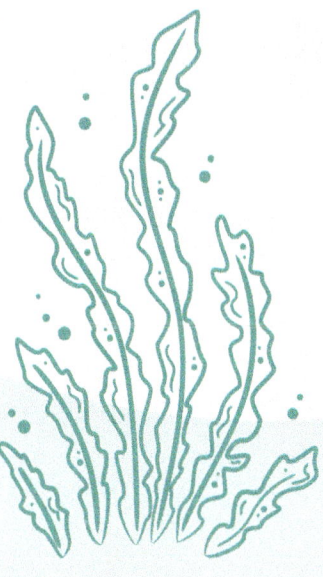

Willing Yourself Out of Narcissistic Abuse

We know from *Swimming with Sharks* that there are three steps to willing yourself out of narcissistic abuse:

Step One: Acknowledge the Reality of the Abuse
Step Two: Want, Choose, and Decide to Make a Change
Step Three: Take Action

Which step are you currently on?

Is there anything preventing you from moving forward? If so, write about it here.

What do you feel like you need in order to move forward?

What are some of the fears you have about moving forward?

Evaluating Your Options

If you've reached Step Three: Take Action, what are the options that you are considering? Are you going to continue treading water, reel yourself out of the water, or keep one foot in and one foot out? Use the prompts below to reflect on this.

Which option are you currently considering?

What are some of your reasons for taking this action right now?

What are some of the fears you have related to taking this action?

What do you fear the narcissist might do?

Take a moment to write about any shame you might be experiencing around taking this action.

Now, ask yourself the following question, and write down your answers below:

What would I do if I weren't afraid?

BOUNDARIES

Remember the first rule of surviving a narcissist?

List some of the narcissistically abusive behaviors that you want to address.

What are some boundaries that you could set to address these behaviors?

When you set these boundaries, what can you say to the narcissist?

Is It Love or Fear?

If you missed chapter 16 in *Swimming with Sharks* because it didn't apply to you, it may be worth going back and reading the short section, "Is It Love or Fear?" This question is the greatest coping mechanism for everything life throws at you, regardless of the context. I use this question to guide my choices throughout every day. Here is an excerpt from chapter 16:

> *What's the best way to model healthy behavior? Focus on love versus fear! Allow love to guide your choices and behaviors, rather than fear. Intentionally guide yourself through this simple process by asking yourself either of the following two questions:*
>
> *Is my reaction rooted in love or fear?*
> *OR*
> *Would this choice be rooted in love or fear?*
>
> *When you allow love to guide your mind over fear, you cannot make the wrong choice. The tricky part is being honest with yourself in identifying when fear has guided you rather than love. Fear has a sneaky way of masking itself for love, especially when it comes to relationships. You may even be thinking, "Alena, you are way off. I'm in this position in the first place because of love, because I chose to love this person who ended up being a narcissist!" I can see where you might think that, but I would argue that if you look closely enough and really examine what led you to stay in that unhealthy relationship, you would be able to see that it was fear, not love.*

So, let's run through some questions to help you start focusing on "Is It Love or Fear?" in your daily life. These do not need to be applicable within the context of your relationship with a narcissist. Take your life as a whole into consideration.

How often do you think you make decisions from fear?

Write down a few examples of the most recent decisions you made from fear.

Which of these decisions could you make from love in the future?

Share a little about your typical reactions to situations and people. Be honest with yourself about when your reactions stem from love and when they stem from fear.

Think of a recent reaction that stemmed from fear. Now imagine what it would be like to repeat that same scenario and instead react from love. Describe exactly what that new experience is like, how does it feel, and how do others respond to you?

Now, think of how others could react to you with love. What kind of a difference would that make in your daily life? How might you feel differently as you go about your day?

Make a list of the people in your life you are going to start reacting to with love.

Think of a simple dilemma you are currently facing or will be facing later today (i.e., what to cook for dinner, whether or not to go for a walk later, etc.). Now, ask yourself which choice(s) will come from love. Write down the answer here.

Example:

Choosing to cook chicken pot pie tonight for dinner will come from a place of love because I know that my kids love it when I cook that.

Going for a walk later will be a loving choice for myself because I know that I will feel good about *me* afterward.

The choice I'm going to make that comes from love is _____

because _____

Continue practicing living from a place of love over fear with little things like this. Before you know it, it will start to feel like second nature and become a natural part of the more challenging aspects of your life!

THE NATURE OF NARCISSISTS

What Species of Shark are You Dealing With?

In chapter 19 of *Swimming with Sharks*, "Shark Species: Types of Narcissists," I give a brief overview of the classifications I find relevant when describing types of narcissists.

*What are your thoughts on the use of the term **Vulnerable** Narcissist?*

What kind(s) of narcissist have you been dealing with? (Overt, covert, malignant, nonmalignant)

What other terms do you think are appropriate to use in identifying the "species" of narcissists you've come across? The Hammerhead Narcissist?

Narcissistic Supply

How do you think that you provide Narcissistic Supply to your narcissist?

Describe how the narcissist in your life uses Narcissistic Supply Hopping.

What kinds of boundaries can you set to limit being used for Narcissistic Supply?

Narcissistic Parents

Which of your parents might be or might have been a narcissist?

How did this affect your childhood?

How has this impacted you as an adult?

How do you think your relationship with them has impacted your current relationships?

Other Narcissists

What other kinds of relationships do you have with potential narcissists?

How can you use this knowledge to help you?

What can you do to mitigate the negative impact they could have on your life?

What kinds of boundaries can you set up?

Escape Preparation: Documentation

This is a continuation of chapter 14, "Prep Step 3: Documentation," from *Swimming with Sharks: Surviving Narcissist-Infested Waters*.

Use the tips here to help you document most effectively and make the most of your new Google account.

In *Swimming with Sharks*, you have access to all the other escape preparation information I share, such as a list of resources and items to gather, suggestions regarding seeking legal counsel and documentation, as well as self-care guidance.

Google Account Creation

Google has many more resources that you can take advantage of than just Gmail! To get started, though, you need to create a new Google account that is private from the narcissist. Keep in mind that the steps I'm outlining below and the tips I share next could change after the printing of this book.

1. Open Chrome.
2. In the top bar, click "File" and then "New Incognito Window." This will ensure there is no history on your computer showing that you even looked at account creation.
    a. If you are using Safari, under "File," it will say "New Private Window."
3. Go to Google.com.
4. Click "Sign In."
5. Click "Create Account."
6. Follow the prompts.
    a. If you have safety concerns, it might be worthwhile to consider using a pseudonym rather than your legal name.
    b. Make sure you use a strong password that the narcissist could not possibly know already or figure out. Using passphrases is typically recommended.
    c. When your browser asks about saving your username and password, make sure you click "No." If you accidentally click "yes," you can always go into your password manager and delete any record of the username and password.
7. Adjust your device settings to limit or completely turn off notifications from appearing or making noise on your phone or computer if there is a risk of the narcissist noticing them.

Google & Mac Tips, Tricks, and Shortcuts

- ⚓ Tip: Always work within a Private or Incognito window to reduce the risk of the narcissist finding what you have done within your history on your computer.
- ⚓ Tip: If you have anything within your history that could cause issues, such as searching for divorce attorneys, make sure you individually delete those items. If you erase all of your history, and that isn't something you usually do, if the narcissist peeks into your history, they'll get suspicious when there isn't anything there.
- ⚓ Tip: Set up multifactor authentication.
    - ⛵ Choose options that would not be accessible to the narcissist, even if they got a hold of your phone.
- ⚓ Tip: Take advantage of the numerous Google applications that can help you right now such as Docs, Sheets, Drive, Keep, Chat, Calendar, and Meet.
- ⚓ Shortcut: To easily access all of the apps, click the group of nine dots at the top right of your screen. A dropdown with shortcuts to the apps will appear.
- ⚓ Tip: You can record voice memos within the Google Keep mobile app by clicking the microphone icon at the bottom of the main page.
- ⚓ Tip: Many of the apps allow you to share or add collaborators to whatever you create with other people.
- ⚓ Trick: When sharing items, sometimes you can adjust the settings to allow the other person to view, comment, or edit. That gives you control over someone else's ability to alter the item or not. This is particularly relevant in Docs and Sheets.
- ⚓ Trick: You can easily share with others by copying and sending a link to the item.
- ⚓ Trick: You can also adjust the visibility of the item from restricted to anyone with the link.
- ⚓ Trick: Rather than texting with your support system, including lawyers, have private conversations with others within Chat. Similarly, in addition to video calls, you can have audio calls within Meet.

- ⚓ Tip: Make sure you carefully adjust your settings to not allow notifications of new chats or incoming calls on your phone if there is a risk of the narcissist seeing.
- ⚓ Trick: Google is fantastic at allowing you to include links almost everywhere. This makes it super easy to share items with others because you don't have to download or attach documents to emails.
- ⚓ Shortcut: To create a hyperlink that allows you to share a link without having to include the entire URL, copy the link first, then highlight any text that you want someone to be able to click in order to access the link (i.e. in an email, a doc, or sheet, etc.), then click insert link, paste the link into the box for the URL and click done.
- ⚓ Shortcut: On a Mac, some useful keyboard shortcuts are:
  - ⛵ Copy: command+C
  - ⛵ Insert link: command+K
  - ⛵ Paste: command+V
  - ⛵ Save: command+S
  - ⛵ Highlight all: command+A
  - ⛵ Delete: command+X
  - ⛵ Go back: command+Z
  - ⛵ Print: command+P
  - ⛵ Bold, Italicize, or Underline: command+B, I, U, respectively
  - ⛵ You can find others or find the shortcuts for other devices by googling "keyboard shortcuts on ____."
  - ⛵ By the way, don't do what I did years ago and keep trying to figure out how to press shift and the equal sign key in order to add the plus sign. The plus (+) signs above stand for "and." You are not supposed to also press the key with the + sign on it. For example, to copy something, press and hold down the "command" key, then press the "C" key.

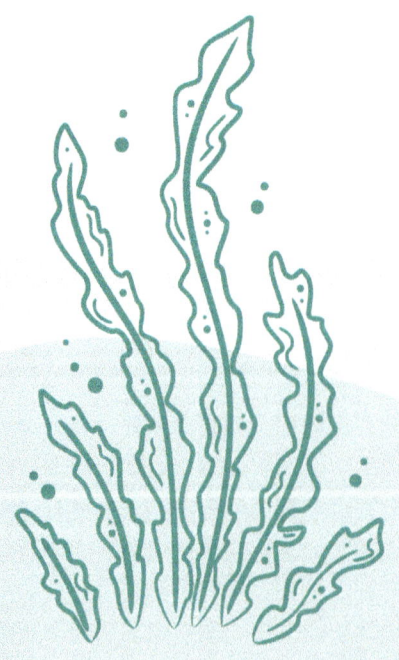

NAVIGATING FORWARD

In *Swimming with Sharks: Surviving Narcissist-Infested Waters*, the section on navigating forward provides information that is unique to what I use therapeutically and teach others and very unlike what you will find elsewhere. For this reason, I encourage you to read "Part 5—Navigating Forward" in *Swimming with Sharks* before completing this section, as it will explain and clarify several parts of the soul-mending process that could otherwise be misleading based on common understanding of the concepts, specifically acceptance and forgiveness.

Soul-Mending: Telling Your Story

The first stage of soul-mending is telling your story. If you haven't already done this, or even if you have but think it will be helpful to do it again, take some time to share your story here. Use extra pages as needed.

Growth

Alena Scigliano

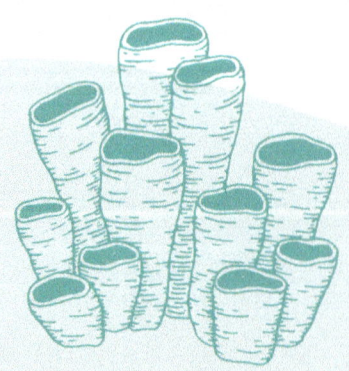

Soul-Mending: Acknowledging the Abuse

What do you associate with the word "abuse"?

What makes it difficult for you to acknowledge that what you've been going through is abuse?

What are you worried other people might think of you?

How do you think being able to use the word "abuse" might change your perspective on yourself, your situation, and/or the narcissist?

Letter to Your Narcissist

This is your opportunity to write anything to your narcissist that you would like to say but would never actually say—or what might be dangerous to say to them. What would you like them to know about how they have impacted you and your life?

GROWTH

Soul-Mending: Growing Your Knowledge and Understanding

What has stood out to you from all the things that you've learned so far about narcissistic abuse?

How has this knowledge already impacted you, or, as you move forward, how do you think your new knowledge will help on the rest of your soul-mending journey?

What would you want others to know?

What do you know now that you wish you had known sooner?

Letter to Your Younger Self

If you could have a conversation with your younger self, what would you say? Are there things you wish you had known sooner? How would you prepare yourself to better handle the narcissistic abuse you've had to endure? Would you warn yourself against your relationship or would you tell yourself to stay because you appreciate the person you are now because of what you've gone through? Or maybe you would want to stay long enough to have your children (if you are in a partnership with a narcissist) but tell yourself to leave right afterward? Whether it's reassurance, resolve, wisdom, love, warnings, or anything else, let it all out here so that you can begin to process through these thoughts.

Growth

Alena Scigliano

Soul-Mending: Retelling Your Story

Now that you've acknowledged the abuse and gained lots of knowledge and understanding about narcissistic abuse, start retelling your story here. Use extra pages as needed.

Growth

Alena Scigliano

Soul-Mending: Acceptance

What are some of the things that you have struggled to accept?

How difficult is it to accept that you don't have control over changing the narcissist?

What are some of the factors that make acceptance difficult?

What would you like to work on accepting?

Letter to Your Current Self

What do you want to say to the person you are now? If you were speaking to a friend, what would you say? What do you want yourself to believe, do, and change? You can say anything, so make the most of this opportunity and be completely honest with yourself. The only restriction I suggest is that you speak with kindness and love to yourself. Do not berate or belittle yourself. You get that enough from the narcissist. Be authentic with your words but find ways to say them that will build you up, not break you down.

Soul-Mending: Forgiveness

What about yourself or the choices you've made would you like to forgive?

What about others and/or the narcissist would you like to be able to forgive?

What are some things that you think you could never forgive?

How do you think it would change you if you could forgive those unforgivable things?

LETTER TO YOUR FUTURE SELF

Take this opportunity to express what you want to make sure your future self remembers. Tell your future self how proud you are of them and specifically name the things you will have accomplished which make you proud. Tell yourself about the kind of person you hope you become, the kinds of relationships you hope you have, and anything else you hope for your future self.

GROWTH

Alena Scigliano

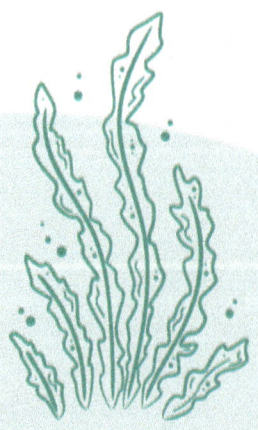

Soul-Mending: Rebuilding Yourself

What are some of the devastating effects that having a relationship (any type) with a narcissist had on you?

How were your self-image, self-esteem, and self-worth impacted?

What would you like to begin believing about yourself?

Remember from *Swimming with Sharks*, healthy self-worth is believing that:

You are worthy just as you are.

You are worthy simply because you exist.

You are worthy of acceptance.

You are worthy of compassion.

You are worthy of kindness.

You are worthy enough to experience joy.

You are worthy of love!

What are some affirmation mantras you can say to yourself?

[ ]

Below are some mantras I frequently use with my patients, as well as for myself.

Worth-related:

I am good enough no matter what!

I am worthy simply because I am. (Or simply because I exist.)

It doesn't matter what anyone else thinks of me!

Acceptance-related:

It's okay that I don't have control.

It's okay that I can't change _____. (Fill in the blank with the narcissist's name.)

It's okay that _____. (Fill in the blank with anything you need to accept.)

An important point I share within therapy is that you do not have to believe these mantras to say them. If you did, you wouldn't need to say them in the first place! And it's okay to feel like you are lying to yourself when you say them. That's normal and how everyone else feels. What you are trying to do here is rewire your brain, creating new neural pathways, by repeatedly inputting new information. A couple of things to keep in mind:

- Make sure it's something you want to believe and that you know is healthy to believe.
- Choose your wording carefully. For example, every word in "It doesn't matter what anyone else thinks of me" was chosen with intention based on not leaving room for ambiguity and what is most effective (i.e.. "I don't care . . ." is not effective in changing your belief system).
- Stick to the same exact wording every time you say it.
- Repeat the mantra every single time you are triggered.
- Set a reminder in your phone with the mantra quoted so that it pops up at least three times per day. And when it does, try not to dismiss it—say it right away.

In *Swimming with Sharks*, I shared:

> The truth is **your worth exists whether you believe in it or not**. It's just that all of the abuse and manipulation caused you to develop a false perception of yourself as unworthy. Once you remember your true self-worth, you'll be able to rediscover, or discover for the first time, your voice, your power, your purpose, and your value. You'll be able to discover what excites you, what brings you joy, and what you're passionate about. This is how you rebuild yourself!

What are some additional ways in which you can work on rebuilding yourself?

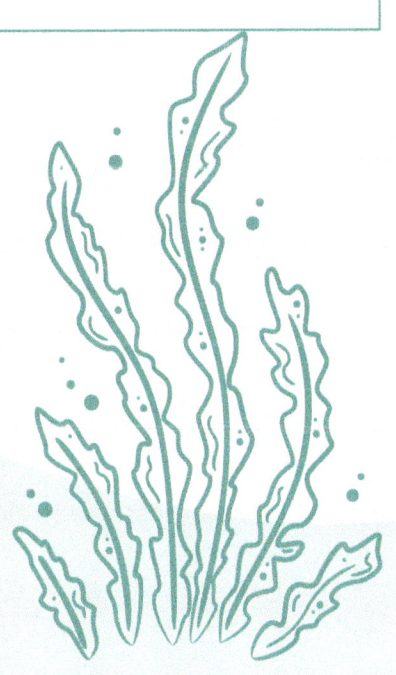

Letter to Someone Else

If there is anyone else you think you would want to share your thoughts with, go ahead and do that here. Maybe it would be helpful to vent to your parents about how you blame them for your situation. Maybe you would like to share some thoughts, feelings, or wisdom with your child(ren). Or perhaps you feel compelled to write a letter to all the other survivor-victims out there, sharing your insights and suggestions. Just like the letter to the narcissist, you don't have to share these unless you really want to.

GROWTH

GROWTH BOOK

Jumping Back In: Triggers

A lot of people develop anxiety triggers as they begin to move forward in their life, independent of the narcissist. Sometimes, the triggers begin to develop even before you separate yourself from them. In fact, these anxieties can often hinder the process of separating, making you doubt how much better things have the chance of being than they are right now.

Make a list of what your current fears are regarding future relationships.

What are you afraid you will find out in the world?

What are you afraid of regarding others?

What are you afraid of regarding yourself?

Jumping Back In: Flags

Let's figure out what the red flags were when you began your relationship with the narcissist. It's not unusual for us to sense that something is off with someone when we are in the beginning of a relationship with them but then brush it off or justify it, rather than heed our intrinsic warning system.

Brainstorm and make a list of anything that seemed off to you the day you first encountered your narcissist.

Brainstorm and make a list of anything that seemed off to you within the first month of your relationship with the narcissist.

Brainstorm and make a list of anything that seemed off to you within the first six months of your relationship with the narcissist.

Oftentimes, the behaviors, traits, etc., that we sense as concerning, but brush off and justify, are actually yellow or red flags that, had we known differently, we would have heeded at the time.

Look back at your lists of what seemed off at the beginning of your relationship. Now, write down the yellow flags—signals that there was something to be concerned about but not clear enough to know for sure that it was going to be such an unhealthy relationship.

Look back again at your list of what seemed off at the beginning of your relationship. Now, write down the red flags — clear signals that the relationship needed to end at that time.

This activity is meant to help you realize that, as you move forward and are faced with the possibility of new relationships, you won't be as helpless as you might feel right now. As you can see, you knew something wasn't right at the beginning of your last relationship with your narcissist. And that was before you had the wisdom to be able to discern what was and wasn't a yellow or red flag. Now that you *are* wiser and stronger, you can rest in the faith of knowing you will be able to perceive, acknowledge, and heed red flags as they come up in the future. You might not notice them immediately, but once you do, you will have the opportunity to remove yourself from an unhealthy relationship.

Now that you've read Swimming with Sharks, *and know more about narcissistic tendencies in general, write down any yellow or red flags that might not have been present in this past relationship but could be in future relationships.*

Jumping Back In: Countertransference as a Red Flag

Sometimes, the red flags are not being waved by the narcissist at all. Sometimes, the brightest red flags are found within ourselves. These often present themselves as our own feelings and thoughts in reaction to a narcissist. Countertransference is a psychology term we use to describe what happens when counselors have a personal reaction within the therapeutic context, often to a patient. Everything in a therapy room provides insight into our work with our patients. While countertransference can provide wisdom into ourselves as therapists, as well as anything we may need to resolve within (i.e., unresolved issues from our own past relationships), it can also provide fantastic insight into who our patients are, what they might be dealing with, or how others may feel around them. This is particularly useful when we are working with patients who have personality disorders. It takes practice and often supervision or consultation, but if we notice that we are getting frustrated, anxious, hurt, angry, etc., in the therapy room, with no obvious explanation for our feelings, that is often insight into the presence of a personality disorder in our patient.

You can use this same concept as you move forward in developing new relationships, to help assuage any fears you have about ending up with other narcissists.

Looking back at your past relationship(s) with a narcissist, what do you remember feeling in reaction to them?

REFLECTION

What emotions did you experience that didn't make sense, but you weren't quite sure what to do with?

```
┌─────────────────────────────────────────────┐
│                                             │
│                                             │
│                                             │
│                                             │
└─────────────────────────────────────────────┘
```

What emotions did you experience that did make sense but that you tried to ignore or blame on yourself?

```
┌─────────────────────────────────────────────┐
│                                             │
│                                             │
│                                             │
│                                             │
└─────────────────────────────────────────────┘
```

SHARK DETECTOR

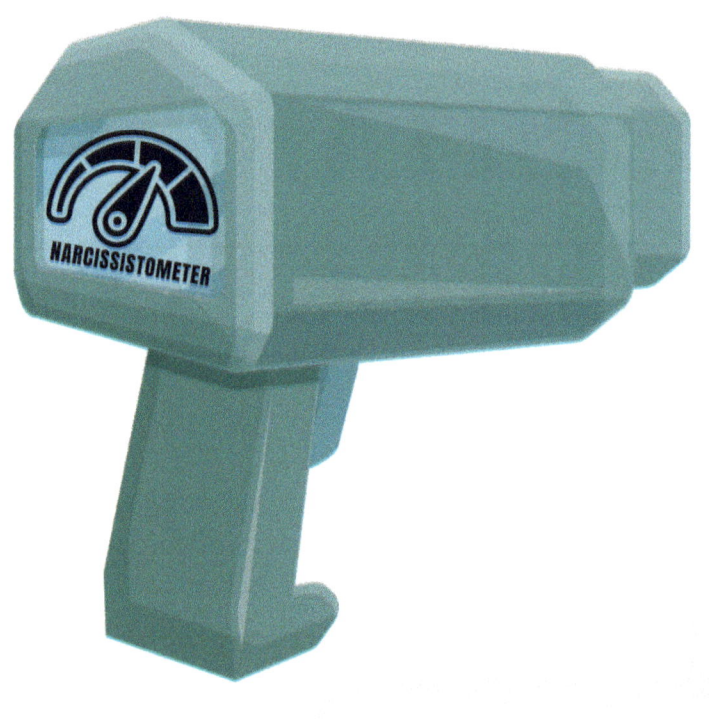

SHARK DETECTOR

The Shark Detector can be used to reflect on the behavior of anyone in your life, whether they are someone you are dating or a random person you encounter at a soccer game. I'm sure an entire book could be filled with examples of red flags, but those I'm sharing here are ones that I've kept track of in my clinical work and personal life. Some of them may not make sense unless you've faced the same thing. But that's a good reflection of what a relationship with a narcissist can be like—the things they do or say leave you scratching your head and saying, "Huh?" because they're completely illogical or irrational. This list will at least give you some common themes to look out for. Some may not be relatable if you haven't experienced them while others may resonate greatly.

As you review the examples below, keep in mind that displaying a couple of these red flags does *not* make someone a narcissist. What *does* indicate that someone is a potential narcissist is noticing a *pattern* of numerous red flags, typically over a period of time. If you only notice one or two early on, keep an eye out for others that may pop up. Red flags don't usually all come out right away, and they don't have to show up around the same time to indicate a pattern.

First Date Dynamics (Romantic or Platonic):

- **What is the flow of the conversation?**
  - ☐ Either making conversation all about theirself or all about you.
  - ☐ Talk constantly without leaving space for you to contribute to the conversation.
  - ☐ Don't ask about you, in a deep way, or at all.
- **Are they really listening to you?**
  - ☐ Not responding to your emotional expression.
  - ☐ Quickly saying okay, gotcha, almost as though cutting off and impatient to move on in the conversation.
  - ☐ Pay attention to the nonverbals of someone who is clearly uninterested.
- **Do they name-drop?**
  - ☐ We all try to impress a person we're on a first date with. The question is, what are we using, doing, or saying to impress the other person?
  - ☐ Try to impress you with who they are or who they've been, or who they've known or met.
  - ☐ Try to impress you with external factors, other than theirselves, not about quality time with self and family.
  - ☐ Kids go to preppy private schools based on school name recognition.
  - ☐ They are all about the names of schools, colleges, universities, corporations, or other organizations.

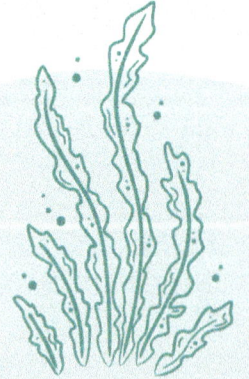

- **Whom are they trying to impress?**
    - ☐ Do they act flirty with the waitress or anyone else?
- **Do they accuse you of anything?**
    - ☐ I've heard of one partner accusing the other on their first date of looking at the waiter like they wanted to sleep with them (however in much more vulgar terms).
- **Do they act one way with you and another way with other people, or the same way with everyone?**
    - ☐ Are they nice to you and mean to others, or vice versa?
    - ☐ Makes you feel like you're special, but then acts similarly to other people in front of you, making you question if you are special to them.
- **Is their behavior condescending?**
    - ☐ Patting the top of the head of another adult.
    - ☐ Speaking to you or someone else as though they are dumb.
    - ☐ Referring to a woman, "She's wife material."
- **Do they seem to have an uncontrollable or awkward need to share what they need/want out of a relationship?**
- **Are they overly doting on you?**
- **Do they repeatedly ignore you?**

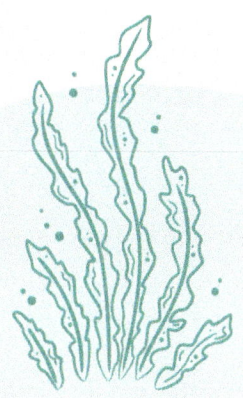
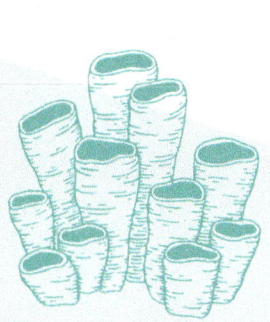

Entitlement:

- Expecting to be treated a certain way based on who they are.
- Belonging to exclusive clubs and organizations.

This isn't Broadway:

- **Does it seem like everything is a show?**
  - Narcissists flaunt who they are and what they've done to make themselves stand out.
  - Really big into their alma maters.
  - Snazzy dressing to get attention.
  - Has lots of parties.
  - A LOT of "friends."
  - Treats everyone like they are family members and can talk to them like they do their actual family members (in a way that's just too much—may seem sincere, but your intuition tells you that something feels off. Or they act the same with everyone, which makes their attitude toward you feel less sincere.)

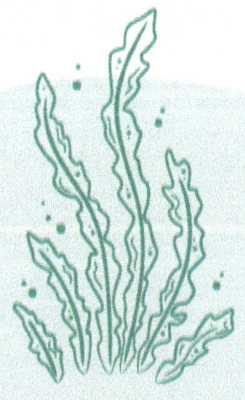

PAST CONFLICT & ADMITTING TO FLAWS/FAULTS OR LAUGHING AT THEIRSELF:

- **Ask how they have resolved previous disputes (don't just look for communication skills, look for someone who admits flaws—this is healthy).**
    - ☐ A narcissist won't admit that they're wrong.
    - ☐ They won't talk about their flaws, failures, or vulnerabilities.
    - ☐ They won't express what their own mistakes were in their past relationships—will blame the exes.

- **Pay attention to whom they blame.**
    - ☐ If they talk about issues at work, are they always blaming someone else?
    - ☐ Can they take responsibility for their own mistakes?

- **Can they laugh at theirself?**
    - ☐ Narcissists typically don't laugh at theirselves and get highly offended and often aggressive when someone teases or pokes fun at them.
    - ☐ Isn't into sarcasm or is uncomfortable with sarcastic jokes that others might make. May be able to dish it out but can't take it.

Trashing Exes:

- **Ask about their previous relationships.**
  - ☐ Talks about exes being super crazy, ridiculing their previous victim—making them seem unreasonable.
  - ☐ Says the ex was too clingy or needy or didn't give them their own space. If they don't see that as being wanted, then that's an issue.
  - ☐ Phone rings while on a date early on in a relationship, you hear someone yelling on the phone. Your date says, "Oh, I don't talk to them. They're crazy."
    - ☐ If you get up and walk out on that date, explaining that you don't get involved with things like that, does the person say to you, "Oh, no one's ever challenged me like that."
  - ☐ They say to you, "I never thought my partner would be strong enough to leave me."
  - ☐ Do they say that all of their exes were broken or damaged?

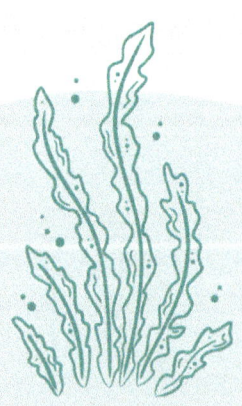

Content of Conversations:

- Is there a negative or positive theme in their conversations?
    - ☐ Gossiping about others.
    - ☐ Critical of others.
    - ☐ Joking of specific groups of people related to firm prejudices and expressing a sense of their own superiority (i.e., racist, sexist, or LGBTQIA+-phobic jokes, among others).
    - ☐ Complains a lot.
    - ☐ Complaining over and over about the amount of work and amount of time spent on something, but they don't do anything to change it and are resistant to any suggestions for change.

Vulnerability:

- **This is going to be your greatest litmus test, not only for gauging how likely someone is to be a narcissist, but also for how ready someone is for a healthy relationship. Because narcissists have such a fragile self-image, being vulnerable is dangerous. It threatens their stability, because vulnerability creates a fear of cracking their foundation and crumbling down. Picture a building after a strong earthquake.**

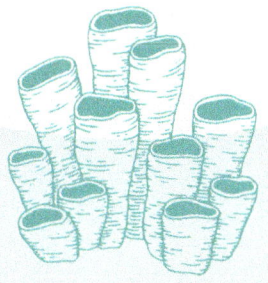

Your Interpersonal Dynamics / Their Response to Your Attention:

- **If you find yourself acting "clingy," pay attention to how they react.**
  - If the person tells you that you are too clingy or needy, leave right away. First of all, think about how they'll be with a child because they are really clingy and needy. And second of all, most healthy people want to spend time with the person they're dating and feel wanted and needed. If they are rejecting your presence or calling you needy, that means that they aren't meeting your needs.
- **Pay attention to their attitude surrounding trust.**
  - Do they expect you to trust them implicitly? Do they make you feel guilty if you question something?
  - Are they quick to mistrust you?
- **Using, "God has been speaking to me," as a means to manipulate and control.**
- **Telling you that you can talk about anything with them and then reacting poorly to what you say or using it against you.**
- **Telling you that "you aren't over your ex."**
- **"It's not my fault you feel that way."**
- **"I'm sorry you feel that way."**

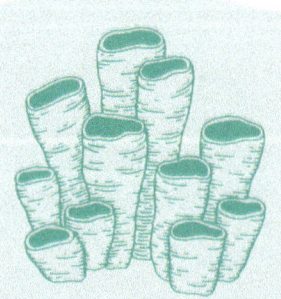

Overly Romantic (Love Bombing):

- **Try saying no!**
  - Pursuing you strongly, even when you say no.
    - Real-life example: Someone said no to a date because they used to date their sister, but the person continued pursuing them in a very pushy way.
    - Sometimes they will react angrily when you say no.
  - They get mad because you cancel or change plans or if you ask them to leave because you need to do something else.
  - They use the shotgun effect. Use every trick in the book until one sticks. All five love languages. Flowers, compliments, quality time, etc.

Family of Origin:

- **Ask about their relationship with their mother/father.**
  - An intense relationship with mother/father—unhealthily strong attachment. Their parent comes before you, particularly if you've committed to one another.
  - Avoids taking you home to meet the family. Or it could be that they introduce you too quickly.

Friends:

- ⊞ **Are you on display or hidden?**
  - ☐ Hiding their relationship status (or hiding it from some people but not others) such as on social media.
  - ☐ The timing of sharing something about your relationship in front of friends is odd.
  - ☐ They'll only come to your place and not invite you to theirs.
- ⊞ **Pay attention to how they are around their friends.**
  - ☐ Showing you off to friends or others right away, and something feels off about it. You might feel like you're being put on display, rather than getting to know friends. Not interested in your opinion of their friends.
  - ☐ If their relationships with their friends seem superficial vs. deep. Meet the guys at the club vs. here are my childhood friends who know and love me.
  - ☐ Sometimes, they won't even introduce you to their friends. This could be because they don't have any (red flag) or it could be because they don't want you to meet them for some reason (red flag).

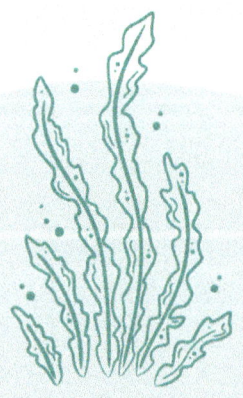

- ☐ The friends they introduce you to, are they social friends, are they work friends (which could say more about them being narcissistic or could be the opposite)—depends on what the introduction is like.
- ☐ Did they talk you up as they introduced you, or did they allow you to talk about yourself?
    - ☐ If they're worried about you making them look bad, they would control the conversation and introduction.
- ☐ Do they stay with you at a party or do they leave you on your own all night? Or, do they seem like they're afraid to leave you alone? Do they get jealous if they see you talking to someone else and react with rage or passive aggression?
- ☐ Do they have their "own friends" that they keep separate and don't integrate with you?

How do they define friendship?
- ☐ A LOT of "friends."
- ☐ Gossiping about others.

How do your friends react to them?
- ☐ Everyone else said that they were an a**hole and didn't understand why you were with them.

How do they treat other people?
- ☐ If they're mean or narcissistically abusive to others, then they can and likely will be that way to you.

Their Personal Identity:

- **How do they seem to define themselves?**
  - By their relationship with others (i.e., Knowing someone else with power or prestige).
  - By their career.
  - By their partner's career (i.e., Behaving as though they are special because they are a spouse of someone with a prestigious career/position).
- **Juniors—naming a child after theirself.**
- **Overly concerned about their looks—everything needs to be perfectly coiffed.**

Careers:

- **Ask about their job/career.**
  - Successful people operate in a world that is rigged for narcissists—so they're often more financially capable of providing.
  - Not doing a job because they love it or because it's their passion or calling. Doing it only because it brings them success and money.

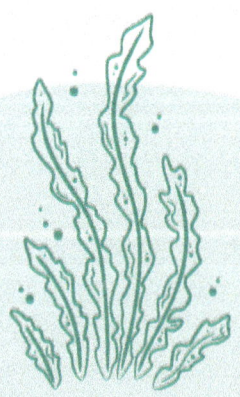

- ☐ If they are in a job and can say that they are successful but not happy — could indicate that they just don't know how to perceive their dreams or have been taught that their dreams are stupid or that they should only pursue a career for "security" to be safe, rather than pursuing for happiness. (This is common for people who aren't narcissists as well, so it would especially need to be considered within the context of a pattern of other red flags.)
- ☐ Jobs that offer power, prestige, or a level of control over others (doctor, lawyer, law enforcement, military, church leader, politician — jobs that have people's lives or well-being in their hands).
- ☐ Not always a narcissist if they enjoy talking about the benefits of their job and how they help people.
- ☐ Seems like they're never satisfied with their job, because it doesn't make them special.

- **Narcissists often name their businesses after themselves.**
- **Believing they are indispensable to their job. "They couldn't do this without me."**
- **Fires or sabotages others for the sake of maintaining control and/or superiority within their company.**

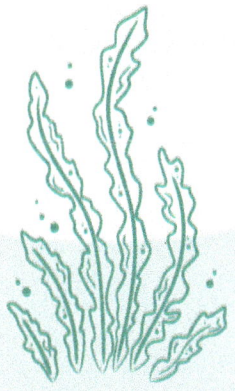

FOR COLLEAGUES OR EMPLOYEES YOU ARE THINKING COULD BE A NARCISSIST:

- Do they have a sudden rage reaction when you inform them of a change they were not anticipating? Keep in mind that "narcissist's rage" does not always take on a boisterous form. Someone can have a rage reaction but still appear relatively calm.
- Do they pay attention while you're talking during a meeting, or do they look at their phone or their laptop?
- Do you catch them rolling their eyes?
- Do they frequently show up late or leave early from meetings?
- Do you get the feeling that they are being one way with you and another way with others? Does their genuineness seem off?
- Do they challenge you during meetings in front of others in a way that doesn't feel quite right to you but also isn't extreme enough for others to notice?
- Do they lie or hide things about their work?
- Do they gaslight you by telling you that they never said something that you know for certain they said?
- Do they agree to make changes but demonstrate a pattern of always returning to their original behavior?

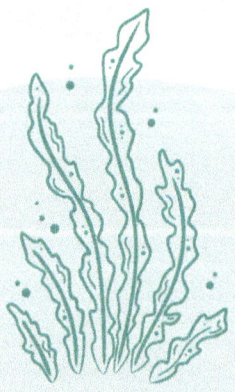

MISCELLANEOUS:

- Seem to thrive on negativity.
- They are a "One-Upper."
- They remember their grandkids' birthdays based on the dates of their surgeries (this was my grandmother).
- Humblebragging.
- Flashy with their material wealth.
- Bragging about the successes or the sacrifices of their parents.

About the Author

As a psychotherapist and Licensed Professional Counselor, Alena Scigliano is one of very few formally trained mental health professionals who specializes in narcissistic abuse. In her private group practice, she provides loving and compassionate psychotherapy to those who are searching for healing from relationships with pathologically narcissistic partners, family members, friends, coworkers, bosses, pastors, and others. In addition, she supports other mental health professionals and organizations through narcissistic abuse education, training, and consultation.

Alena's personal mission is to inspire others to live with love, joy, compassion, and kindness by empowering them to choose love over fear in every facet of their life. As the founder and CEO of a multistate group practice, she has built a team of psychotherapists who are dedicated to improving the lives of hundreds of people every month. Passionate about innovating the business of counseling, Alena offered teletherapy long before COVID, and has developed innovative forms of therapy such as "Beach & Talk Therapy" and "Indoor Walk & Talk Therapy." Alena also provides consultation to other group practice owners in order to help them improve the systems and processes operating their businesses.

Alena's mental health career was inspired by the powerful changes her own counseling journey made in her life. Therapy helped her learn that even though she and her parents shared a loving relationship, she didn't have the power to stop their alcohol abuse. In addition, it helped her let go of a lifetime of learned fear and anxiety in order to raise her own children in a much healthier environment based on love, joy, and patience. Alena enjoys sharing the difference that unschooling (an unstructured and self-directed type of homeschooling) made in her children's education and their journeys to discovering their individual selves. She passionately advocates for allowing children to hold onto their innate love of learning by embracing their individual learning styles and believes that we succeed as parents if our children know how to learn, grow up feeling loved and accepted, and know how to love, accept, and show compassion toward themselves and others.

www.ingramcontent.com/pod-product-compliance
Lightning Source LLC
Chambersburg PA
CBHW061120070526
44583CB00028B/3351